WOK COOKBOOK

WOK COOKBOOK

TYPHOON

First published in 2002
for Typhoon International
by Hamlyn,
a division of Octopus Publishing Group Limited
2–4 Heron Quays, London, E14 4JP

ISBN 0 600 60636 8

Printed in China

ACKNOWLEDGEMENTS
Octopus Publishing Group Limited/Jean Cazals 11/Sandra Lane back cover, 51,
55/Neil Mersh front cover bottom right, 19, 31, 35/Peter Myers front cover
top, front cover bottom left, front cover bottom centre, 15, 23, 27, 39, 43, 47,
59, 63/Sean Myers 3/Philip Webb 7

NOTES

1 Eggs should be large unless otherwise stated. This book contains some dishes
made with raw or lightly cooked eggs. It is prudent for more vulnerable people,
such as pregnant and nursing mothers, invalids, the elderly, babies and young
children, to avoid uncooked or lightly cooked dishes made with eggs.

2 Both metric and imperial measures have been given in all recipes. Use one set of
measurements only and not a mix of both.

3 Meat and poultry should be cooked thoroughly. To test if poultry is cooked,
pierce the flesh through the thickest part with a skewer or fork—the juices should
run clear, never pink or red. Keep refrigerated until ready for cooking.

4 This book includes dishes made with nuts and nut derivatives. It is advisable for
those with known allergic reactions to nuts and nut derivatives and those who
may be potentially vulnerable to these allergies, such as pregnant and nursing
mothers, invalids, the elderly, babies, and children, to avoid dishes made with
nuts and nut oils. It is also prudent to check the labels of preprepared ingredients
for the possible inclusion of nut derivatives.

Contents

WOK COOKBOOK

Stir-frying is a cooking technique which has long been used throughout South-East Asia and is now very popular in Western cooking, too. This is partly because it is a quick and simple way to cook foods, ideally suited to people with busy lifestyles, but also because it is a very healthy form of cooking, during which meat, fish, rice and vegetables lose very few important minerals and vitamins.

Stir-frying involves cooking food very quickly in oil heated to a high temperature, with seasonings and optional sauces, stocks and wine. Since the amount of oil used in most stir-frying recipes is minimal, it is a technique which could more properly be described as 'cooking with oil', rather than 'cooking in oil'.

You will find in this book a wide and deliciously varied selection of wok and stir-fry recipes, many of them based on the different cooking styles of South-East Asia, from China to Malaysia, and with others showing a distinctive Western influence on the choice of ingredients.

Using a wok

While stir-frying can be done successfully in a heavy-based frying pan, the ideal utensil is the widely used Asian cooking pan, the wok, which can also be used for steaming, braising and deep-frying. The wok's curved sides allows food to be pushed up the sides and out of the oil, which drains off the food and back to the bottom of the wok, while the food still cooks in the heat of the pan.

In the Western kitchen the wok is most easily used on gas cookers, because the heat can be adjusted much more quickly than on electric ones. If you think you will be doing a lot of wok cookery, it is a good idea to have two woks, a big, 14 inch one with a lid for deep-frying and steaming, and a smaller, 12 inch one for stir-frying. You will be using both hands when stir-frying, one to hold the wok's handle, and the other to stir the food constantly with a spatula or chopsticks as it cooks.

Wok cookery utensils

Besides the wok itself, other useful utensils to have when cooking with a wok, include a tempura rack, which fits on to the wok rim to hold pieces of food during cooking and to drain food once it has been cooked; a slotted spoon or skimmer for lifting cooked foods out

of the wok; and several wooden spatulas (or chopsticks) for stirring the food in the wok. Thai cooks also have a large mesh skimmer, for lowering foods into hot oil for deep-frying.

For preparing food for wok cookery, you should have one or two solid wooden chopping boards; several good sharp knives, including a thin bladed knife for shredding, slicing and dicing, a cleaver for cutting meat very finely and a knife for cutting through the bones and joints of poultry; and a pestle and mortar so that you can have a supply of freshly ground spices at all times.

Preparing a new wok

While nonstick and stainless steel woks are available, the traditional Chinese wok, made of carbon steel, is still the most popular among dedicated stir-fry cooks. A new carbon steel wok is always sold coated with lacquer to stop it rusting. To prepare it for use, you must remove this film:

• Heat the wok over a high heat until it is very hot indeed, then scrub it in warm, soapy water with a stiff brush and rinse it thoroughly. Dry the wok by putting it over a moderate heat.

• Now you must season the wok, to prevent it rusting and to stop food sticking to it during cooking. To do this, simply wipe over the entire inside surface of the dry wok with a pad of kitchen paper soaked in cooking oil.

• To preserve the seasoning, do not wash the wok in detergent after use. Use just hot water, plus a stiff brush or non-abrasive scourer to scrape off any food stuck to the base. Repeat the seasoning process after washing the wok, so that it develops a natural nonstick surface.

Successful stir-frying

• Foods must be properly prepared in advance, trimmed and cut into similarly sized and shaped pieces so that they cook evenly.

• The wok should be preheated before the oil, which should be a good quality light oil. Heat the oil until it is smoking, allow it to cool slightly (until it is sizzling), then add the food.

• Keep the heat high during cooking, so that the overall cooking time is a short one.

• Ingredients which need longer cooking should be put into the wok first: for this reason, you should carefully follow the order of cooking set out in the recipes in this book.

• The food should be stirred and moved vigorously in the wok all the time it is cooking, using chopsticks or a spatula.

• Never over-cook stir-fried food: it should be tender but still with a crisp texture, and a fresh colour. Serve it as soon as it is ready.

Garnishing wok and stir-fry dishes

Many different garnishes, including fresh herbs, nuts, seeds and vegetable pieces have been used to make simple yet effective finishing touches for the recipes in this book. To extend the Far Eastern style of your cooking, try using these typical oriental garnishes.

Red Chilli Flowers

Using a sharp, pointed knife, cut the chilli lengthways into 4 sections, slicing from the base to the tip, being careful not to cut right through the base. With the point of the knife, scrape out the chilli seeds, then drop the chillies into a bowl of iced water and place in the refrigerator for at least 30 minutes, until the sections of the chilli open out like a flower. Drain well before use.

Cucumber or Lemon Slices

Very thin cucumber and lemon slices, used either flat or as curls, make an attractive garnish. Use the notch on a canelle knife to remove strips of skin at regular intervals down a cucumber or lemon before cutting them into even, thin slices. (Remove any pips from lemon slices.) For curls, make a cut from the edge of the slice to the centre, then twist the two cut edges away from each other.

Radish Roses

Remove the stalk from the radish and, using the point of a small sharp knife, cut a row of petal shapes round the radish, keeping them joined at the base. Cut a second row of petal shapes in between and above the first row. Continue cutting rows of petal shapes until you reach the top of the radish. Place the radish rose in iced water for several hours to open out.

Spring Onion Tassels

Using a small sharp knife, remove and discard the root from the spring onion and trim the stem to about 7.5 cm (3 inches) long. Cut lengthways through the green stalk several times to within 4 cm (1½ inches) of the end. Place in iced water for about 1 hour to open out.

Tomato Rose

Use a firm tomato to make this garnish. With a sharp knife, remove the skin in one continuous strip about 1 cm (½ inch) wide, starting at the smooth end. With the flesh side inside, start to curl the strip of tomato skin from the base end, forming a bud shape. Continue winding the strip of skin into a rose.

GARLIC MIXTURE

This is a condiment which Thai cooks use a great deal. It has a great flavour and is extremely useful.

2 tablespoons crushed garlic
2 tablespoons chopped coriander root or stalk
½ tablespoon pepper

Put all the ingredients into a mortar and pound with a pestle until they are thoroughly blended and form a paste. If you like, it can be stored, covered, in the refrigerator for 1–2 days until required. This will enhance its flavour.

COCONUT MILK AND CREAM

Coconut milk is not the liquid inside a fresh coconut. It comes from the flesh of the coconut, infused in hot water. If the coconut 'milk' is left to stand, a thicker 'cream' rises to the top. Both coconut milk and cream are readily available in supermarkets and Oriental stores.

To make your own, mix 900 ml (1½ pints) water and 400 g (13 oz) grated or desiccated coconut in a saucepan. Bring the mixture to the boil, lower the heat and simmer, stirring occasionally, until the mixture is reduced by one-third. Strain, squeezing out as much liquid as possible. Pour the strained milk into a bowl and chill in the refrigerator. When it is cold, skim off the thicker cream that has risen to the surface.

CHICKEN STOCK

This recipe makes a good amount of stock. It can be kept in an air-tight container for up to 3 days in the refrigerator. If you prefer, it can be made in advance and frozen; it will keep in the freezer for 3 months.

1 Put a 1 kg (2 lb) chicken (giblets reserved) in a large saucepan with 2.5 litres (4 pints) water. Add the giblets (except the liver which would make the stock taste bitter), 1 onion and 1 carrot, both quartered, 1–2 celery sticks, sliced, 1 large bouquet garni, 6 black peppercorns and a pinch of salt. Bring to the boil, skimming off the scum as it rises to the surface.
2 Lower the heat, half cover the pan and simmer gently for 3 hours. Skim and top up the water as necessary.
3 Remove the bird and strain the stock into a bowl. Blot off any surface fat with kitchen paper and use as needed.

FISH STOCK

This stock is quick to prepare and well worth making for its extra flavour. Do not cook it for longer than the time stated, or it will taste bitter. It can be kept in an air-tight container for up to 24 hours in the refrigerator. If you prefer, it can be made in advance and frozen; it will keep in the freezer for 3 months.

1 Put 500 g (1 lb) fish trimmings into a saucepan with 900 ml (1½ pints) water, 2 tablespoons chopped onion, 2 tablespoons chopped celery, a handful of parsley, 2 bay leaves, 1 teaspoon black peppercorns and 2–3 tablespoons dry white wine.
2 Bring slowly to the boil, skim off any scum forming on the surface. Half cover the pan and simmer for 25 minutes.
3 Strain the stock through a fine sieve and use as required.

VEGETABLE STOCK

Another quickly made stock, this stock can be kept in an air-tight container for up to 3 days in the refrigerator. If you prefer, it can be made in advance and frozen; it will keep in the freezer for up to 3 months.

1 Heat 4 tablespoons of sunflower oil in a heavy-based saucepan. Add 2 garlic cloves, 2 chopped onions and 2 sliced leeks. Fry gently for 10 minutes.
2 Add 2 diced potatoes, 4 chopped carrots and 4 sliced celery sticks. Fry for a further 10 minutes.
3 Add 4 chopped ripe tomatoes to the saucepan with 125 g (4 oz) mushrooms, 125 g (4 oz) rice, a bouquet garni and 1.8 litres (3 pints) water. Bring to the boil and simmer for 30 minutes.
4 Strain the stock through a fine sieve and use as required.

EGG DROP SOUP

This well-known Chinese soup is easily prepared; the wok is ideal for this because it gives a large surface area of soup into which the beaten egg can be swirled. The success of this soup depends on the quality of the stock, so don't try to cut corners by using a stock cube.

10 spring onions
2 tablespoons chopped coriander leaves
900 ml (1½ pints) Chicken Stock
(see page 10)
about 4 tablespoons soy sauce
2 teaspoons cornflour
1 tablespoon cold water
2 eggs
salt and pepper

1 Chop 6 of the spring onions and mix them with the coriander. Shred the remaining 4 spring onions.

2 Pour the stock into a wok and heat it through, then stir in the soy sauce, tasting the soup as you do so, and add salt and pepper to taste. The soup will need some pepper but, depending on the strength of the soy sauce, it may not need any salt. Blend the cornflour with the water and stir this into the hot soup, then bring the soup to the boil to thicken it slightly.

3 Beat the eggs thoroughly without allowing them to become frothy – the idea is to combine the yolks and whites evenly. Stir the spring onion and coriander mixture into the soup, bring it to a rapid boil and stir the soup so that it swirls around vigorously in the wok. Immediately turn off the heat and pour in the beaten egg in a slow thin stream. It should set in the swirling soup to give thin strips. Serve immediately, garnished with the remaining spring onions.

Serves 4
Preparation time: 15 minutes
Cooking time: 5–7 minutes

PUMPKIN SOUP

1 teaspoon finely sliced lemon grass or
¼ teaspoon grated lemon rind
1 teaspoon finely sliced root ginger
1 tablespoon basil leaves
½ green pepper, cored, deseeded and
chopped
3 kaffir lime leaves or ¼ teaspoon grated
lime rind
100 ml (3½ fl oz) water
1 tablespoon groundnut oil
2 garlic cloves, finely chopped
10 shallots, thinly sliced
1 teaspoon crushed dried chillies
1 small red chilli, chopped
500 ml (17 fl oz) Vegetable Stock
(see page 10)
50 g (2 oz) French beans, chopped
3 tablespoons Thai fish sauce or soy sauce
750 g (1½ lb) pumpkin, peeled and cubed
1 teaspoon sugar
1 teaspoon ground white pepper
1 tablespoon crunchy peanut butter
3 teaspoons curry powder
175 ml (6 fl oz) coconut milk
2 teaspoons cornflour
basil leaves, to garnish

1 Blend the lemon grass or lemon rind, ginger, basil, green pepper, lime leaves or lime rind and water in a food processor or blender, then strain the mixture and throw way the liquid, reserving the purée.

2 Heat the oil in a large wok. Add the garlic, shallots and dried and fresh chillies and stir-fry over a high heat for 1 minute.

3 Add the purée, 400 ml (14 fl oz) of the stock, the French beans, fish sauce or soy sauce and pumpkin. Stir over a moderate heat. Add the sugar, pepper, peanut butter and curry powder and stir again. When the pumpkin is tender, after about 10 minutes, add the coconut milk and bring to a hard boil for 1 minute.

4 Blend the remaining stock with the cornflour until smooth, add it to the soup and stir to thicken.

5 Ladle the soup into a large warmed serving bowl and garnish with the basil.

Serves 4
Preparation time: 30 minutes
Cooking time: 15 minutes

BEAN THREAD NOODLE SOUP

2 tablespoons vegetable oil
2 teaspoons Garlic Mixture (see page 9)
250 g (8 oz) minced pork
1 litre (1¼ pints) Chicken Stock
(see page 10)
125 g (4 oz) bean thread noodles
4 spring onions, cut into 2.5 cm (1 inch)
lengths
½ onion, finely chopped
2 tablespoons Thai fish sauce
2 tablespoons salt
250 g (8 oz) large raw prawns, peeled and
deveined
2 celery sticks with leaves, sliced
pepper

1 Heat the oil in a wok, add the garlic mixture and stir-fry for 1 minute.

2 Add the minced pork and stir-fry for 3 minutes, then pour in the stock and bring to the boil. Stir in the noodles, spring onions, onion, fish sauce and salt. Bring the soup back to the boil and cook for 3 minutes. Lower the heat, add the prawns and celery and simmer for a further 2 minutes.

3 Transfer the soup to a warmed serving bowl, season with pepper and serve immediately.

Serves 4
Preparation time: 10 minutes
Cooking time: 10 minutes

CRISPY SEAWEED

750 g (1½ lb) spring greens
vegetable oil, for deep-frying
1½ teaspoons caster sugar
1 teaspoon salt

1 Separate the leaves of the spring greens. Wash them well and then pat dry with kitchen paper or a clean tea towel.

2 Using a very sharp knife, shred the spring greens into the thinnest possible shavings. Spread out the shreds on kitchen paper and leave for about 30 minutes, until thoroughly dry.

3 In a wok, heat the oil for deep-frying to 180–190°C (350°–375°F), or until a cube of bread browns in 30 seconds. Turn off the heat for 30 seconds, then add a small batch of shredded spring greens. Turn up the heat to moderate and deep-fry the greens until they begin to float. Take care as they tend to spit while they are cooking.

4 Remove the greens with a slotted spoon and drain on kitchen paper. Cook the remaining greens in batches in the same way. When they are all cooked, transfer to a bowl and sprinkle with the sugar and salt. Toss gently to mix and serve warm or cold.

Serves 8
Preparation time: 10 minutes, plus drying
Cooking time: 10 minutes

THAI PRAWN TOASTS

These delicious toasts can be eaten on their own, but a few mooli and green pepper strips make an attractive accompaniment. Mooli is from the same vegetable family as the radish, which can be used instead, but it is much larger and has a slightly less peppery taste.

75 g (3 oz) raw prawns, peeled, deveined and minced
125 g (4 oz) minced pork
1 tablespoon finely chopped coriander leaves, plus extra to garnish
1 tablespoon finely chopped spring onion
1 teaspoon Garlic Mixture (see page 9)
1 tablespoon Thai fish sauce
1 egg, beaten
5 slices white bread
5 tablespoons sesame seeds
vegetable oil, for deep-frying

TO SERVE (OPTIONAL):
plum sauce
¼ green pepper, very thinly sliced
wide strips of raw mooli

1 Put the minced prawns and pork into a bowl with the coriander leaves, spring onion, garlic mixture and fish sauce. Add the egg and mix well.

2 Cut each slice of bread into 4 pieces of roughly equal size. Spread each piece of bread with some of the pork and prawn mixture, using a knife to press the mixture firmly on to the bread. Sprinkle the sesame seeds on top.

3 Pour about 2.5 cm (1 inch) of oil into a wok and heat to 180–190°C (350–375°F) or until a cube of bread browns in 30 seconds. Add the pieces of bread, a few at a time, with the topping side facing downwards. Cook over a moderate heat for 6–8 minutes, then turn over the bread and cook the other side until golden.

4 Remove with a slotted spoon, drain on kitchen paper, garnish with coriander and serve hot with plum sauce, very thin slices of pepper and strips of mooli.

Serves 4
Preparation time: 20 minutes
Cooking time: 15–20 minutes

SPRING ROLLS

250 g (8 oz) spring roll wrappers, each 12 cm (5 inches) square
I egg, beaten
oil, for deep-frying

FILLING:
2 tablespoons vegetable oil
2 tablespoons Garlic Mixture (see page 9)
125 g (4 oz) crab meat
125 g (4 oz) raw prawns, peeled and finely chopped
125 g (4 oz) minced pork
125 g (4 oz) vermicelli, soaked and cut into I cm (½ inch) lengths
125 g (4 oz) mushrooms, chopped
2 tablespoons Thai fish sauce
2 tablespoons light soy sauce
I teaspoon sugar
5 spring onions, finely chopped

TO GARNISH:
I large red chilli, cut into matchstick strips
I lime, sliced
basil leaves

I First make the filling. Heat the oil in a wok, add the garlic mixture and stir-fry for 1 minute until golden brown. Add the crab meat, prawns and pork and stir-fry for 10–12 minutes, or until lightly cooked. Add the vermicelli, mushrooms, fish sauce, soy sauce, sugar and spring onions and stir-fry for a further 5 minutes until all the liquid has been absorbed. Set aside to cool.
2 Separate the spring roll wrappers and spread them out under a clean tea towel to keep them soft. Put about 2 tablespoons of the filling in the centre of one edge of each spring roll wrapper, and brush the left and right edges with beaten egg.
3 Fold the sides over the filling and then roll up like a sausage. Brush the top edge with more beaten egg and then seal. Keep the filled rolls covered while you make the remaining spring rolls in the same way.
4 Heat the oil in a wok and cook the spring rolls, a few at a time, for 5–8 minutes, or until golden brown. Turn them once during cooking so that they brown evenly. Drain on kitchen paper and serve hot, garnished with strips of red chilli, slices of lime and a few basil leaves.

Serves 6
Preparation time: 25 minutes
Cooking time: 20–25 minutes

LEMON CHICKEN

This classic dish, which originated in Hong Kong, is simplicity itself to make. Spring onions are included to add crunch to the dish, but they are not essential. If you prefer, you can use green pepper instead, or leave out the vegetables altogether.

I egg white
2 teaspoons cornflour
pinch of salt
2 boneless, skinless chicken breasts, cut into thin strips across the grain
300 ml (½ pint) vegetable oil
½ bunch of spring onions, shredded
I garlic clove, crushed
lemon slices, to garnish

SAUCE:
2 teaspoons cornflour
cold Chicken Stock (see page 10) or water
finely grated rind of ½ lemon
2 tablespoons lemon juice
I tablespoon soy sauce
2 teaspoons rice wine or dry sherry
2 teaspoons caster sugar

I First prepare the sauce. Mix the cornflour to a thin paste with the stock or water, then stir in the remaining sauce ingredients. Set aside.

2 Lightly beat the egg white in a shallow dish with the cornflour and salt. Add the strips of chicken and turn to coat. Set aside.

3 Heat the oil in a wok until hot but not smoking. With a fork, lift the chicken strips one at a time out of the egg white mixture and drop them into the hot oil. Shallow-fry them in batches for about 3–4 minutes, or until golden, then remove with a slotted spoon and drain on kitchen paper. Keep hot.

4 Pour off all but 1 tablespoon of the oil from the wok. Add the spring onions and garlic and stir-fry over a moderate heat for 30 seconds. Stir the sauce, pour into the wok and stir to mix. Increase the heat to high and bring to the boil, stirring constantly.

5 Return the chicken to the wok and stir-fry for 1–2 minutes or until evenly coated in the sauce. Serve immediately, garnished with lemon slices.

Serves 2
Preparation time: 20 minutes
Cooking time: about 25 minutes

THAI GREEN CHICKEN CURRY

2 tablespoons groundnut oil
2.5 cm (1 inch) piece of fresh root ginger, peeled and finely chopped
2 shallots, chopped
4 tablespoons Thai green curry paste
625 g (1¼ lb) boneless, skinless chicken thighs, cut into 5 cm (2 inch) pieces
300 ml (½ pint) coconut milk
4 tablespoons Thai fish sauce
1 teaspoon palm sugar or soft brown sugar
3 kaffir lime leaves, finely chopped, or ¼ teaspoon grated lime rind
1 green chilli, deseeded and finely sliced
salt and pepper
fried chopped garlic, to garnish
rice sticks, to serve (optional)

1 Heat the oil in a wok. Add the ginger and shallots and stir-fry over low heat for about 3 minutes or until softened. Add the curry paste and fry for 2 minutes.

2 Add the chicken to the wok, stir until evenly coated in the spice mixture and fry for 3 minutes to seal the chicken pieces. Stir in the coconut milk and bring the curry to the boil. Reduce the heat and cook the curry over a low heat, stirring occasionally, for about 10 minutes or until the chicken is cooked through and the sauce has thickened.

3 Stir in the fish sauce, sugar, kaffir lime leaves and chilli. Cook the curry for a further 5 minutes, then add salt and pepper to taste. Garnish the curry with fried garlic and serve rice sticks as an accompaniment, if liked.

Serves 4
Preparation time: 10 minutes
Cooking time: 25 minutes

GINGER CHICKEN WITH HONEY

This dish tastes even better if it is cooked a day in advance and then thoroughly reheated
before serving.

2 tablespoons vegetable oil

3 boneless, skinless chicken breasts, chopped

3 chicken livers, chopped

1 onion, finely sliced

3 garlic cloves, crushed

2 tablespoons dried black fungus (cloud's ears), soaked in hot water for 20 minutes

2 tablespoons soy sauce

1 tablespoon clear honey

25 g (1 oz) piece of fresh root ginger, peeled and finely chopped

5 spring onions, chopped

1 red chilli, finely sliced into strips, to garnish

rice sticks, to serve (optional)

1 Heat the oil in a wok then add the chicken breasts and livers. Fry the chicken mixture over a moderate heat for 5 minutes, then remove it with a slotted spoon and set aside.

2 Add the onion to the wok and fry it gently until soft, then add the garlic and the drained mushrooms and stir-fry for 1 minute. Return the chicken mixture to the wok.

3 Stir together the soy sauce and honey in a bowl until blended, then pour the mixture over the chicken and stir well. Add the ginger and stir-fry for 2–3 minutes. Finally, add the spring onions. Serve immediately, garnished with red chilli strips and accompanied by rice sticks, if liked.

Serves 4
Preparation time: 15 minutes, plus soaking
Cooking time: 10–15 minutes

HONEY-SOY DUCK BREASTS WITH PLUM AND MANGO SALSA

4 duck breasts
2 tablespoons dark soy sauce
I tablespoon clear honey
I teaspoon grated fresh root ginger
I teaspoon chilli powder

PLUM AND MANGO SALSA:
I large ripe mango, peeled, stoned and finely diced
6–8 plums, stoned and finely diced
grated rind and juice of I lime
I small red onion, finely chopped
I tablespoon olive oil
I tablespoon roughly chopped mint leaves
I tablespoon roughly chopped coriander
salt and pepper

1 Use a sharp knife to score the skin on the duck breasts lightly, cutting down into the fat but not through to the meat.

2 Heat a wok until very hot, then place the duck breasts in it, skin sides down, and cook for 3 minutes, until sealed and browned. Turn the breasts over and cook for a further 2 minutes. Using a slotted spoon, transfer the duck breasts to a baking sheet, arranging them skin sides up.

3 Mix the soy sauce, honey, ginger and chilli powder in a small bowl. Spoon this mixture over the duck and cook in a preheated oven, 200°C (400°F), Gas Mark 6, for 6–9 minutes, until cooked to your liking. The duck may be served pink in the middle or more thoroughly cooked.

4 Meanwhile, combine all the ingredients for the salsa in a bowl and season well.

5 Thinly slice the cooked duck and fan out the slices slightly on individual plates. Spoon some of the salsa over the duck and serve immediately, offering the remaining salsa separately.

Serves 4
Preparation time: 15 minutes
Cooking time: 11–14 minutes

SWEET AND SOUR PORK

250 g (8 oz) pork, cut into cubes
I teaspoon salt
1½ tablespoons brandy
I egg, beaten
I tablespoon cornflour
vegetable oil, for deep-frying
125 g (4 oz) canned bamboo shoots, drained and cut into chunks
I green pepper, cored, deseeded and cut into chunks
2 spring onions, cut into 2.5 cm (1 inch) lengths
425 g (14 oz) can pineapple chunks in juice, drained and juice reserved

SAUCE:
3 tablespoons vinegar
3 tablespoons sugar
½ teaspoon salt
I tablespoon tomato purée
I tablespoon soy sauce
I tablespoon cornflour
I teaspoon sesame oil

1 Place the pork in a bowl and sprinkle with the salt and brandy. Leave to marinate in the refrigerator for 15 minutes, then add the beaten egg and cornflour and mix well.

2 Heat the oil in a wok to 180–190°C (350–375°F), or until a cube of bread browns in 30 seconds. Deep-fry the pork for 3 minutes. Remove the wok from the heat but leave the pork in the oil for a further 2 minutes, then remove it with a slotted spoon and drain on kitchen paper. Return the wok to the heat and reheat the pork with the bamboo shoots for 2 minutes. Remove and drain on kitchen paper.

3 Pour off the excess oil, leaving 1 tablespoonful in the wok. Add the green pepper and spring onions. Mix all the sauce ingredients with a little canned pineapple juice and add to the wok, stirring until thickened. Add the pork, bamboo shoots and pineapple and serve hot.

Serves 3–4
Preparation time: 15 minutes, plus marinating
Cooking time: 15 minutes

PORK WITH CHILLI AND BASIL

2 tablespoons vegetable oil
1 garlic clove, crushed
2 chillies, finely chopped, or to taste
125 g (4 oz) pork fillet, finely sliced
¼ teaspoon pepper
1 tablespoon Thai fish sauce
½ teaspoon sugar
50 g (2 oz) canned bamboo shoots, very finely sliced (optional)
2 tablespoons finely chopped onion
2 tablespoons finely sliced red pepper
4 tablespoons Chicken or Vegetable Stock (see page 10)
2 handfuls of basil, plus extra to garnish
3–4 large red chillies, sliced, to garnish
boiled rice, to serve

1 Heat the oil in a wok. Add the garlic and chillies and stir-fry until the garlic is just golden. Add the pork, pepper, fish sauce and sugar, stirring constantly.

2 Stir in the bamboo shoots, if using, with the onion, red pepper and stock. Cook for 5 minutes. Stir in the basil leaves and cook for 1 minute more. Garnish with the extra basil leaves and large slices of red chilli. Serve immediately with boiled rice.

Serves 4
Preparation time: 10 minutes
Cooking time: 8–10 minutes

LAMB WITH OKRA AND TOMATOES

250 g (8 oz) small okra, trimmed
3 tablespoons vegetable oil
1 onion, thinly sliced
1–2 garlic cloves, crushed
2 teaspoons ground coriander
2 teaspoons turmeric
1 teaspoon hot chilli powder, or to taste
500 g (1 lb) lamb fillet, cut into thin strips across the grain
250 g (8 oz) ripe tomatoes, skinned and roughly chopped
finely grated rind and juice of ½ lemon
½ teaspoon caster sugar
salt

1 Blanch the okra in lightly salted boiling water for 5 minutes, then drain, rinse under cold running water and drain again. Set aside.

2 Heat the oil in a wok over a moderate heat. Add the onion, garlic, coriander, turmeric and chilli powder and stir-fry for 2–3 minutes or until the onion is softened, taking care not to the let the onion brown.

3 Add the lamb strips to the wok, increase the heat to high and stir-fry for 3–4 minutes or until the lamb is browned on all sides.

4 Add the tomatoes and stir-fry until the juices run, then add the lemon rind and juice, sugar, and salt to taste. Stir-fry to mix, then add the okra and toss for 3–4 minutes or until heated through. Serve hot.

Serves 3–4
Preparation time: 15 minutes
Cooking time: about 20 minutes

BEEF WITH CASHEW NUTS

500 g (1 lb) lean fillet steak, thinly sliced into strips
2 tablespoons soy sauce
1 tablespoon dry sherry
3 tablespoons sesame oil
3 tablespoons water
2 teaspoons cornflour
1 tablespoon finely chopped fresh root ginger
2 garlic cloves, crushed
125 g (4 oz) unsalted roasted cashew nuts
3 celery sticks, sliced diagonally
salt and pepper

1 Place the fillet steak in a bowl and add the soy sauce, sherry, 2 teaspoons of the sesame oil, the water, cornflour, ginger and salt and pepper. Cover and leave to marinate in the refrigerator for at least 20 minutes.

2 Heat the remaining oil in the wok. Remove the strips of steak from the marinade and stir-fry quickly in the hot oil for 2 minutes until brown and sealed on the outside. Remove with a slotted spoon and set aside. Reserve the marinade.

3 Add the garlic, cashew nuts and celery to the wok and stir-fry quickly over a moderate heat for 2–3 minutes, tossing well.

4 Return the steak to the wok with the reserved marinade and mix well with the nuts and celery. Increase the heat and continue cooking, stirring all the time, until the sauce thickens. Transfer to a warmed serving dish and serve immediately.

Serves 3–4
Preparation time: 10 minutes, plus marinating
Cooking time: 8 minutes

SESAME PRAWNS WITH PAK CHOI

600 g (1 lb 3 oz) raw tiger prawns, peeled
but with the tails left on
1 teaspoon sesame oil
2 tablespoons light soy sauce
1 tablespoon clear honey
1 teaspoon grated fresh root ginger
1 teaspoon crushed garlic
1 tablespoon lemon juice
500 g (1 lb) pak choi
2 tablespoons vegetable oil
salt and pepper

1 Put the prawns into a bowl. Add the sesame oil, soy sauce, honey, ginger, garlic and lemon juice. Season with salt and pepper and mix well, then set aside to marinate for 5–10 minutes.

2 Bring a large saucepan of water to a rolling boil. Cut the heads of pak choi in half lengthways, then blanch them in the boiling water for 40–50 seconds. Drain well, cover and keep warm.

3 Heat the oil in a large wok. Add the prawns with their marinade and stir-fry briskly for 3–4 minutes or until the prawns are pink and just cooked through.

4 Divide the pak choi among 4 plates and serve immediately with the prawns and any juices from the pan.

Serves 4
Preparation time: 15 minutes, plus marinating
Cooking time: 4–5 minutes

PRAWNS IN COCONUT SAUCE

16 large raw prawns, peeled and deveined
2 tablespoons vegetable oil
1 large onion, finely chopped
2 stalks lemon grass, chopped
2 red chillies, deseeded and sliced
2.5 cm (1 inch) piece of fresh root ginger, peeled and shredded
1 tablespoon ground cumin
1 tablespoon ground coriander
2 tablespoons Thai fish sauce
250 ml (8 fl oz) thick coconut milk
3 tablespoons roasted peanuts, coarsely ground
2 tomatoes, skinned and chopped
1 teaspoon sugar
juice of ½ lime, to serve
coriander leaves, to garnish

1 Rinse the prawns under cold running water, then pat dry on kitchen paper. With a sharp pointed knife, slit along the undersides from head to tail.

2 Heat the oil in a wok. Add the onion and fry until soft and golden. Add the lemon grass, red chillies, ginger, cumin and coriander, and stir-fry for 2 minutes.

3 Add the fish sauce and coconut milk to the wok. Stir well and then add the peanuts and chopped tomatoes. Cook gently over a low heat until the tomatoes are soft and the flavours of the sauce are well developed.

4 Stir in the prawns and simmer gently for 5 minutes, or until the prawns are pink and tender. Stir in the sugar, then transfer to a serving dish. To serve, sprinkle with lime juice and garnish with coriander leaves.

Serves 4
Preparation time: 20 minutes
Cooking time: 17–20 minutes

GINGER AND SPRING ONION CRAB

2 tablespoons sherry

1 tablespoon chicken stock or water

2 tablespoons cornflour

1 large crab, chopped into serving pieces, with claws and legs cracked open

3 tablespoons vegetable oil

4 slices fresh root ginger, peeled and finely chopped

4 spring onions, finely chopped

1 teaspoon salt

1 tablespoon soy sauce

2 teaspoons sugar

1 Mix 1 tablespoon of the sherry with the stock or water and cornflour. Pour over the crab and leave to marinate for a few minutes.

2 Heat the oil in a wok until it is very hot. Add the crab and fry briskly for about 1 minute, turning the pieces in the oil. Add the ginger, spring onions, salt, soy sauce, sugar and the remaining sherry. Cook for about 5 minutes, stirring all the time. Add a little water if the mixture becomes very dry. Serve immediately.

Serves 2

Preparation time: 20 minutes

Cooking time: 8–10 minutes

PRAWN AND CRAB CAKES WITH CHILLI JAM

250 g (8 oz) white crab meat
grated rind and juice of 1 lime
4 spring onions, finely chopped
1 red chilli, deseeded and finely chopped
1 teaspoon grated fresh root ginger
1 teaspoon crushed garlic
3 tablespoons chopped coriander leaves
3 tablespoons mayonnaise
125 g (4 oz) fresh white breadcrumbs
200 g (7 oz) peeled cooked tiger prawns,
roughly chopped
salt and pepper
oil, for shallow frying
coriander leaves, to garnish
crisp rocket salad or green salad, to serve
(optional)

CHILLI JAM:
2 red chillies, deseeded and finely diced
6 tablespoons sugar
2 tablespoons water

1 Put the crab meat, lime rind and juice, spring onions, chilli, ginger, garlic, chopped coriander, mayonnaise and breadcrumbs in a food processor or blender and process until well mixed. Turn the mixture into a bowl and fold in the prawns with salt and pepper to taste. Cover and chill while making and cooling the chilli jam.

2 To make the chilli jam, place all the ingredients in a small saucepan and heat gently until simmering. Cook for 4–5 minutes, until the sugar has dissolved and the mixture has thickened slightly. Set aside to cool.

3 Divide the prawn mixture into 12 equal-sized portions. Use your hands to roll a portion into a ball, then flatten it into a cake. Repeat with the remaining portions of mixture.

4 Heat the oil in a wok and fry the cakes for 3–4 minutes on each side or until golden. Drain on kitchen paper and serve immediately, garnished with coriander leaves. Serve the chilli jam spooned over the cakes or separately. A crisp rocket salad or green salad is a good accompaniment.

Serves 4
Preparation time: 15 minutes, plus cooling
Cooking time: 15 minutes

SAUTÉ OF SCALLOPS WITH MANGETOUT

8 shelled scallops with coral, defrosted and
dried thoroughly if frozen
3 tablespoons vegetable oil
6 spring onions, thinly sliced on the
diagonal, plus extra to garnish
2.5 cm (1 inch) piece of fresh root ginger,
peeled and finely chopped
175 g (6 oz) mangetout, trimmed
1 garlic clove, crushed
1 tablespoon sesame oil
2 tablespoons soy sauce
½ teaspoon caster sugar
pepper

1 Slice the scallops thickly, detaching the corals and keeping them whole. Set the corals aside.

2 Heat 2 tablespoons of the vegetable oil in the wok over a moderate heat. Add the spring onions and ginger and stir-fry for a few seconds. Add the mangetout and garlic and stir-fry for 2 minutes, then tip the vegetable mixture into a bowl and set aside.

3 Heat the remaining vegetable oil with the sesame oil over a moderate heat. Add the sliced scallops and stir-fry for 3 minutes. Return the spring onion, ginger and mangetout mixture to the wok, add the reserved corals, soy sauce and sugar and increase the heat to high. Toss for 1–2 minutes or until all the ingredients are combined and piping hot. Season with pepper to taste and serve immediately, garnished with spring onions.

Serves 2
Preparation time: 15 minutes
Cooking time: about 10 minutes

FISH WITH BLACK BEAN SAUCE

Black bean sauce, which is rich and delicious, is a traditional accompaniment to fish and chicken in oriental dishes. Salted black beans are small and wrinkled with a pungent, salty taste. They are sold in oriental supermarkets or delicatessens in packets or they are sometimes described as fermented beans and sold in cans.

sesame oil, for frying
25 g (1 oz) piece of fresh root ginger, peeled and cut into fine strips
1 large garlic clove, chopped
3 tablespoons salted black beans
1 tablespoon lemon juice
2 tablespoons soy sauce
2 teaspoons sugar
150 ml (¼ pint) dry sherry
750 g (1½ lb) thick white fish fillet (such as cod, haddock or coley), in 2 pieces, skinned
4 large spring onions, finely sliced diagonally, plus extra to garnish
1 red pepper, cored, deseeded, grilled and cut into fine strips, to garnish
rice noodles, to serve (optional)

1 Heat a little sesame oil in a wok and add the ginger, garlic and black beans. Stir-fry for 2 minutes, then stir in the lemon juice, soy sauce, sugar and sherry.

2 Place the fish fillets in the sauce in the wok. Simmer gently for 20–25 minutes, by which time the fish should be cooked through. Sprinkle the spring onions over the top of the fish, cook for just a few minutes longer, then transfer the fish and sauce to a warm serving dish or, alternatively, divide the fish into 4 pieces and serve on individual plates. Serve immediately with rice noodles, if liked, and garnished with the red pepper strips and spring onions.

Serves 4
Preparation time: 15 minutes
Cooking time: 25–30 minutes

FISH IN GARLIC SAUCE

I mullet, lemon sole or John Dory, cleaned
oil, for deep-frying
3 tablespoons vegetable oil
2 tablespoons Garlic Mixture (see page 9)
2 tablespoons Thai fish sauce
I teaspoon sugar
2 celery sticks, thinly sliced

TO GARNISH:
coriander sprigs
I red chilli, thinly sliced

1 Neatly score the skin of the fish diagonally in both directions to let the sauce penetrate during cooking. Pat dry with kitchen paper. Heat the oil for deep-frying in a wok or large saucepan and deep-fry the fish for 10–15 minutes until golden brown. Using a slotted spoon, carefully remove the fish from the wok and drain on kitchen paper.

2 Heat the vegetable oil in a wok large enough to hold the fish in a single layer. Stir in the garlic mixture and cook until it changes colour. Add the fish sauce and stir in the sugar. Add the fish to the pan, turning it until well coated.

3 Transfer the fish to a serving dish and keep warm. Add the celery to the sauce remaining in the pan and stir-fry for 2 minutes, then pour the mixture over the fish. Garnish with coriander sprigs and strips of red chilli. Serve warm.

Serves 4
Preparation time: 15 minutes
Cooking time: 20 minutes

SPICY GREEN BEANS WITH SHALLOTS

3 tablespoons vegetable oil
2 garlic cloves, crushed
2 shallots, thinly sliced
1 slice fresh root ginger, peeled and chopped
1 red chilli, deseeded and finely chopped
½ teaspoon salt
500 g (1 lb) green beans, trimmed and cut into 5 cm (2 inch) lengths
50 g (2 oz) unsalted cashew nuts
125 ml (4 fl oz) Chicken Stock (see page 10)
2 tablespoons dry sherry
1 tablespoon light soy sauce
1 teaspoon vinegar
1 teaspoon sugar
black pepper

1 Heat the oil in a wok. Add the garlic, shallots and ginger and stir-fry briskly over a moderate heat for 1 minute. Stir in the red chilli and salt and continue stir-frying for 30 seconds.

2 Add the green beans and cashew nuts to the wok and toss well to combine with the garlic, shallots and spices. Stir-fry quickly for 1 minute to brown the cashew nuts.

3 Add the chicken stock, dry sherry, soy sauce, vinegar and sugar and bring to the boil. Reduce the heat slightly and continue stir-frying for about 4 minutes, stirring and turning, until the beans are cooked and the liquid has thickened. Turn into a warmed serving dish and serve immediately, seasoned with a generous sprinkling of black pepper.

Serves 4
Preparation time: 10 minutes
Cooking time: 8–10 minutes

CHINESE BRAISED VEGETABLES

5–6 Chinese dried mushrooms, soaked in
warm water for 20 minutes
250 g (8 oz) firm tofu, cut into cubes
4 tablespoons vegetable oil
125 g (4 oz) carrots, sliced
125 g (4 oz) mangetout, trimmed
125 g (4 oz) Chinese leaves, shredded
2 spring onions, cut into 1.25 cm
(½ inch) lengths
125 g (4 oz) canned bamboo shoots,
drained and sliced
1 teaspoon sugar
1 tablespoon light soy sauce
1 teaspoon cornflour
1 tablespoon cold water
1 teaspoon sesame oil
salt

1 Drain the dried mushrooms and squeeze them dry. Discard the hard stalks and cut the caps into thin slices.

2 Bring a saucepan of lightly salted water to the boil and add the tofu. Boil for 2–3 minutes until firm. Remove the cubes with a slotted spoon and drain well on kitchen paper.

3 Heat about half of the oil in a wok. Add the tofu and fry until lightly browned on all sides. Remove with a slotted spoon and set aside. Heat the remaining oil in the wok. Add the vegetables and stir-fry for 2 minutes. Stir in the tofu with 1 teaspoon salt, the sugar and soy sauce. Cover, reduce the heat and braise for 3 minutes.

4 Meanwhile, mix the cornflour to a smooth paste with the water. Stir into the braised vegetables in the wok. Increase the heat and continue stirring until the sauce thickens. Sprinkle in the sesame oil and serve immediately.

Serves 4
Preparation time: 15 minutes, plus soaking
Cooking time: 15 minutes

OKRA WITH TOMATOES

75 g (3 oz) clarified butter (ghee) or 25 g
(1 oz) butter mixed with 2 tablespoons
vegetable oil
4 green cardamom pods, split open
1 small onion, finely sliced
500 g (1 lb) okra, trimmed
500 g (1 lb) tomatoes, skinned and
quartered
1 teaspoon garam masala
salt and pepper
2 tablespoons chopped coriander leaves,
to garnish
poppadums, to serve (optional)

1 Heat the clarified butter or butter and oil mixture in a wok and add the cardamoms. Fry these for a few seconds, then add the onion, season with a little salt and pepper and cook for about 5 minutes, until soft but not browned. Add the okra and tomatoes and cook for about 5 minutes, stirring the vegetables frequently. The okra should be tender, but take care not to overcook them because, in a fairly dry dish of this type, they can become slimy and unpleasant in texture.

2 As soon as the vegetables are cooked, sprinkle on the garam masala, garnish with chopped coriander and serve immediately with poppadums, if liked.

Serves 4
Preparation time: 15 minutes
Cooking time: about 12 minutes

Vegetables in Oyster Sauce

3 tablespoons vegetable oil
1 garlic clove, crushed
125 g (4 oz) cabbage, shredded
125 g (4 oz) cauliflower florets
½ teaspoon pepper
2 tablespoons oyster sauce
150 ml (¼ pint) Chicken or Vegetable
Stock (see page 10)
125 g (4 oz) broccoli, separated into
florets
2 carrots, cut into fine strips
125 g (4 oz) mushrooms, thinly sliced
1 onion, sliced into rings
50 g (2 oz) bean sprouts
shredded carrot, to garnish
boiled white rice, to serve

1 Heat the oil in a wok. Add the crushed garlic and stir-fry quickly over a moderate heat until golden. Do not allow it to get too brown.

2 Add the shredded cabbage and cauliflower florets and season with the pepper. Stir in the oyster sauce and the stock and cook, stirring constantly, for 3 minutes.

3 Add the broccoli, carrots, mushrooms and onion to the wok together with the bean sprouts. Stir-fry for 2 minutes. Transfer the fried vegetables to a large warmed dish, garnish with shredded carrot and serve immediately with rice.

Serves 4
Preparation time: 15 minutes
Cooking time: 7–8 minutes

BRAISED AUBERGINES

vegetable oil, for frying
4 spring onions, sliced
4 garlic cloves, sliced
2.5 cm (1 inch) piece of fresh root ginger, peeled and finely sliced
2 large aubergines, cut into 5 cm (2 inch) strips
2 tablespoons soy sauce
2 tablespoons dry sherry
2 teaspoons chilli sauce

TO GARNISH:
1 red chilli, deseeded and chopped
1 green chilli, deseeded and chopped

1 Heat 2 tablespoons of oil in a wok. Add the spring onions, garlic and ginger and stir-fry for about 30 seconds. Remove the mixture from the wok and set aside.

2 Increase the heat, add the aubergines and stir-fry until they are browned, adding more oil as necessary. Using a slotted spoon, remove the aubergines and drain on kitchen paper.

3 Pour off the oil from the wok. Return the spring onions, garlic, ginger and aubergine to the wok. Add the soy sauce, sherry and chilli sauce, stir well and cook for 2 minutes.

4 Spoon the aubergines into a warmed serving dish, garnish with red and green chillies and serve immediately.

Serves 4–6
Preparation time: 15 minutes
Cooking time: 7–10 minutes

HOT THAI BEEF SALAD

This contrast of fiery hot meat and refreshing, colourful fruit looks great and tastes wonderful. Thai food is usually hot and chillies are a favourite ingredient, but if you prefer a milder taste, include only a few of the chilli seeds, or even none at all.

2 tablespoons vegetable oil

500 g (1 lb) rump or fillet steak, cut across the grain into thin strips

3 garlic cloves, finely chopped

2 green chillies, finely sliced into rings

juice of 2 lemons

1 tablespoon Thai fish sauce

2 teaspoons caster sugar

2 ripe papayas, peeled and finely sliced

½ large cucumber, cut into matchstick strips

75 g (3 oz) bean sprouts

1 head crisp lettuce, shredded

chilli sauce, to serve (optional)

1 Heat a wok, add the oil and place over a moderate heat until hot. Add the steak, garlic and chillies, increase the heat to high and stir-fry for 3–4 minutes or until the steak is browned on all sides. Pour in the lemon juice and fish sauce, add the sugar and stir-fry until sizzling.

2 Remove the wok from the heat. Lift the steak out of the liquid with a slotted spoon and toss with the papayas, cucumber, bean sprouts and lettuce. Drizzle the liquid from the wok over the salad ingredients as a dressing and serve hot, with a bowl of chilli sauce if liked.

Serves 4
Preparation time: 20 minutes
Cooking time: 5–10 minutes

ARTICHOKE AND RED PEPPER STIR-FRY

Roasted red pepper is soft and sweet, with a smoky 'barbecue' flavour.

1 large red pepper
2 tablespoons olive oil
1 onion, finely chopped
2.5 cm (1 inch) piece of fresh root ginger,
peeled and finely chopped
1 garlic clove, crushed
300 g (10 oz) can artichoke hearts,
drained and sliced
1 tablespoon balsamic vinegar
salt and pepper
basil leaves, to garnish

1 Roast the red pepper under a hot grill, turning it frequently until the skin is charred black on all sides. Wrap the pepper in kitchen paper, put it in a polythene bag and seal tightly. Leave until cold.
2 Unwrap the red pepper and rub off the blackened skin under cold running water. Pull out and discard the core and seeds, then cut the pepper open lengthways, rinse and pat dry with kitchen paper. Cut the pepper lengthways into thin strips, then set aside.
3 Heat the oil in a wok over a moderate heat. Add the onion, ginger and garlic and stir-fry for 2–3 minutes or until softened, taking care not to let the mixture brown. Add the artichokes and pepper strips, increase the heat to high and toss until piping hot. Sprinkle over the balsamic vinegar and add salt and pepper to taste. Serve immediately, garnished with basil leaves.

Serves 4
Preparation time: about 20 minutes, plus cooling
Cooking time: about 15 minutes

PRAWN AND WHITE CABBAGE SALAD

300 g (10 oz) white cabbage, finely sliced
3 tablespoons vegetable oil
1 tablespoon sliced shallots
1 garlic clove, crushed
1 tablespoon chopped dried red chillies
1 tablespoon Thai fish sauce
1½ tablespoons lemon juice
1 tablespoon roughly chopped roasted peanuts
4 tablespoons coconut cream
10 cooked tiger prawns, peeled, deveined and halved lengthways
250 g (8 oz) sliced roast pork
salt

1 Put the cabbage in a saucepan of boiling water and cook over a high heat for 2 minutes. Drain the cabbage in a colander, refresh it under cold running water then return it to the pan and heat it through.

2 Heat the oil in a wok. Add the shallots and stir-fry for 2 minutes, then, with a slotted spoon, transfer them to kitchen paper to drain. Add the garlic to the oil remaining in the wok and fry over a gentle heat until just golden. Drain on kitchen paper as for the shallots. Cook and drain the red chillies in the same way, adding more oil if necessary.

3 Transfer the cabbage to a large bowl, add the fish sauce, lemon juice, peanuts, coconut cream, prawns and sliced pork. Season with salt to taste, then mix well. Spoon the salad on to a warm serving platter, sprinkle with the stir-fried shallots, garlic and chillies, and serve immediately.

Serves 4
Preparation time: 20 minutes
Cooking time: 10–15 minutes

EGG-FRIED NOODLES

4 tablespoons groundnut oil
1 garlic clove, crushed
1 shallot, thinly sliced
125 g (4 oz) fresh egg noodles
grated rind of 1 lime
2 teaspoons soy sauce
2 tablespoons lime juice
125 g (4 oz) chicken breast or pork fillet,
sliced
125 g (4 oz) prepared squid or crab meat
125 g (4 oz) raw prawns, peeled
and deveined
1 tablespoon yellow soya bean paste
1 tablespoon Thai fish sauce
2 tablespoons palm sugar or soft
brown sugar
2 eggs
2 red chillies, deseeded and chopped
pepper

TO GARNISH:
coriander leaves
lime rind, finely sliced

1 Heat half of the oil in a wok, add the garlic and shallot and stir-fry quickly until golden and tender.

2 Plunge the egg noodles into boiling water for a few seconds. Drain well and then add to the wok. Stir-fry with the grated lime rind, soy sauce and lime juice for 3–4 minutes. Remove, drain and keep warm.

3 Add the remaining oil to the wok together with the chicken or pork, squid or crab meat and the prawns. Stir-fry over a high heat until cooked. Season with pepper and stir in the soya bean paste, fish sauce and sugar.

4 Break the eggs into the wok and stir gently until the mixture sets. Add the chillies and season to taste with salt and pepper. Mix in the noodles and warm through over a low heat. Serve garnished with coriander leaves and lime rind.

Serves 4
Preparation time: 10 minutes
Cooking time: 20 minutes

CHOW MEIN

This dish, which literally translated means 'stir-fried noodles', is well known to everyone
who eats in Chinese restaurants. Originally invented by Chinese immigrants to the USA,
these noodles are now cooked all over the Western world, and with almost any meat,
fish or vegetable added to them – there are no hard-and-fast rules for making chow mein.

250 g (8 oz) Chinese rice noodles
2 tablespoons vegetable oil
3–4 spring onions, thinly sliced on the
diagonal
2.5 cm (1 inch) piece of fresh root ginger,
peeled and finely chopped
1 garlic clove, crushed
2 boneless, skinless chicken breasts, cut
into thin strips across the grain
125 g (4 oz) mangetout, trimmed
125 g (4 oz) sliced, cooked lean ham,
shredded
75 g (3 oz) bean sprouts
pepper

SAUCE:
2 teaspoons cornflour
8 tablespoons cold Chicken Stock
(see page 10)
2 tablespoons soy sauce
2 tablespoons rice wine or dry sherry
2 teaspoons sesame oil

1 Cook the rice noodles according to packet instructions. Drain the noodles, rinse under cold water and set aside.

2 To prepare the sauce, put the cornflour into a bowl and mix to a paste with 2 tablespoons of the stock. Stir in the remaining stock, the soy sauce, rice wine or sherry and the sesame oil. Set aside.

3 Heat the oil in a wok over moderate heat. Add the spring onions, ginger and garlic and stir-fry for 1–2 minutes or until softened, taking care not to let them brown. Add the chicken, increase the heat to high and stir-fry for 3–4 minutes or until lightly coloured on all sides.

4 Add the mangetout and stir-fry for 1–2 minutes or until just tender, then add the ham and bean sprouts and stir-fry to combine. Stir the sauce, pour it into the wok and bring to the boil, stirring constantly. Add the drained noodles and toss until combined and piping hot. Season with pepper to taste and serve immediately.

Serves 4
Preparation time: 30 minutes
Cooking time: about 15 minutes

NOODLES WITH CRAB SAUCE

150 g (5 oz) egg noodles
2 tablespoons vegetable oil
125 g (4 oz) spinach or cabbage, roughly chopped
125 g (4 oz) drained canned crab meat
1 teaspoon soy sauce
250 ml (8 fl oz) Chicken Stock (see page 10)
1 spring onion, finely chopped, to garnish

1 Cook the egg noodles according to packet instructions until just tender but still firm. Drain well, then transfer to a warmed serving dish. Set aside in a warm place while you prepare the sauce.

2 Heat the oil in a wok and add the crab meat and spinach or cabbage. Stir-fry for 1 minute.

3 Add the soy sauce and stock to the wok and cook briskly for 2–3 minutes, stirring occasionally. Pour the crab sauce over the warm egg noodles and garnish with chopped spring onion. Serve immediately.

Serves 2–3
Preparation time: 10 minutes
Cooking time: 15 minutes

VERMICELLI NOODLES WITH SAUCE

500 g (1 lb) dried rice vermicelli
125 g (4 oz) ready-fried tofu, sliced
1 tablespoon Thai red curry paste
50 g (2 oz) piece of fresh root ginger,
peeled and chopped
250 ml (8 fl oz) Coconut Milk (see page 9)
1½ teaspoons salt
300 ml (½ pint) hot water
2 teaspoons sugar

TO GARNISH:
chopped coriander leaves
sliced ready-fried tofu
1 red chilli, finely sliced

1 Soak the vermicelli in a bowl of warm water for 15–20 minutes.
2 Meanwhile, put the tofu, curry paste, ginger, coconut milk and salt into a food processor or blender and process until smooth. Add the hot water and process again for 5 seconds. Pour the mixture into a wok and bring to the boil, stirring continuously. Lower the heat to a simmer and add the sugar. Continue cooking gently for 3–4 minutes.
3 Drain the vermicelli and place in a serving bowl. Pour the sauce over it and sprinkle with coriander leaves, tofu slices and chilli slices.

Serves 4–6
Preparation time: 10 minutes, plus soaking
Cooking time: 10 minutes

COCONUT RICE

450 ml (¾ pint) Coconut Milk (see page 9)
½ teaspoon turmeric
375 g (12 oz) basmati rice, washed and drained
8 small onions, roughly chopped
20 peppercorns
1 teaspoon salt

TO GARNISH:
finely chopped spring onions
toasted coconut slivers (optional)

1 Put the coconut milk in a wok, stir in the turmeric, then add the rice. Bring to the boil, then cover and simmer gently for about 5 minutes. Add the onions, peppercorns and salt and continue cooking gently for another 10 minutes or until the rice is tender. Be careful not to let the rice burn.

2 Transfer the rice to a warmed serving dish and garnish with chopped spring onions and coconut slivers, if liked.

Serves 4
Preparation time: 10 minutes
Cooking time: 15 minutes

SPECIAL EGG-FRIED RICE

2–3 eggs
2 spring onions, finely chopped, plus extra to garnish
2 teaspoons salt
3 tablespoons vegetable oil
125 g (4 oz) cooked peeled prawns
125 g (4 oz) cooked meat, such as chicken or pork, diced
50 g (2 oz) canned bamboo shoots, drained and diced
4 tablespoons frozen peas, cooked
1 tablespoon light soy sauce
375–500 g (12 oz–1 lb) cold cooked rice

1 Break the eggs into a small bowl, add 1 teaspoon of the finely chopped spring onions and a pinch of the salt and beat lightly with a fork.

2 Heat about 1 tablespoon of the oil in a wok and add the beaten egg mixture. Stir constantly until the eggs are scrambled and set. Remove the scrambled eggs from the wok and set aside in a bowl.

3 Heat the remaining oil in the wok, and add the prawns, meat, bamboo shoots, peas and the remaining chopped spring onions. Stir-fry briskly for 1 minute, and then stir in the soy sauce.

4 Stir-fry for 2–3 minutes and then add the cooked rice, breaking it up, together with the scrambled eggs and the remaining salt. Stir well to break up the scramble eggs into small pieces and separate the grains of rice. Serve hot, garnished with spring onions.

Serves 4
Preparation time: 10 minutes
Cooking time: 8–10 minutes

CRISPY RICE WITH DIPPING SAUCE

When boiling rice, Thai cooks reserve the layer of sticky grain left in the bottom of the saucepan to make this dish.

250 g (8 oz) glutinous rice
vegetable oil, for deep-frying

DIPPING SAUCE:
125 ml (4 fl oz) coconut milk
50 g (2 oz) minced pork
50 g (2 oz) cooked peeled prawns, minced
1 teaspoon Garlic Mixture (see page 9)
1½ tablespoons Thai fish sauce
1½ tablespoons sugar
50 g (2 oz) onion, finely chopped
50 g (2 oz) roasted peanuts, crushed

1 Put the rice into a saucepan and pour in water to cover it. Bring to the boil, cover the pan and simmer until the rice is thoroughly cooked and sticky. Drain the rice in a sieve. Spread the rice in a layer, as thinly as possible, on greased baking sheets, pressing down well. Set aside to dry in a warm place or in an oven at 120°C (250°F), Gas Mark ½.

2 Meanwhile, make the dipping sauce. Pour the coconut milk into a wok and bring slowly to the boil. Add the minced pork and prawns, stirring to break up any lumps. Mix in the garlic mixture, fish sauce, sugar, chopped onion and roasted peanuts. Reduce the heat and simmer the sauce for 20 minutes, stirring occasionally.

3 When the rice is completely dry and firm, remove it from the baking sheets with a spatula and break it into pieces about 7–10 cm (3–4 inches) across.

4 Heat the oil for deep-frying to 180–190°C (350–375°F), or until a cube of bread browns in 30 seconds, and deep-fry the rice pieces until golden. You should hear the grains beginning to pop in about 5 seconds. Remove from the oil with a slotted spoon and drain on kitchen paper.

5 Pour the dipping sauce into a bowl and serve with the crispy rice pieces.

Serves 4
Preparation time: 15 minutes
Cooking time: 25 minutes

NASI GORENG

250 g (8 oz) long-grain rice
750 ml (1¼ pints) water
2 eggs
2½ tablespoons vegetable oil
I small onion, roughly chopped
2 garlic cloves, roughly chopped
I fresh green chilli, deseeded and roughly chopped
I cm (½ inch) terasi (shrimp paste) or 1–2 teaspoons anchovy essence
I teaspoon tomato purée
250 g (8 oz) boneless cooked lean chicken, pork or beef, cut into thin strips
250 g (8 oz) cooked peeled prawns, defrosted and dried thoroughly if frozen
about 3 tablespoons soy sauce
salt and pepper

TO GARNISH:
fried onion rings
coriander sprigs
few cucumber slices

1 Rinse the rice under cold running water, then put it into a saucepan. Add the measured water, season to taste with salt and bring to the boil. Stir once, cover and simmer for 12–15 minutes, or until the water is absorbed. Remove the pan from the heat, tip the rice into a sieve and rinse under cold running water. Set aside.
2 Beat the eggs and season to taste. Heat 1½ teaspoons of the oil in an omelette pan, add the eggs and make an omelette in the usual way. Slide the omelette on to a board and roll it up tightly. Set aside. Pound the onion, garlic, chilli and terasi or anchovy essence, if using, to a paste using a pestle and mortar, or process in a food processor until smooth.
3 Heat the remaining oil in a wok over a moderate heat. Add the onion mixture and tomato purée and stir-fry for 2–3 minutes, taking care not to let the mixture brown.
4 Add the meat, increase the heat and stir-fry for 1–2 minutes or until hot. Add the prawns and stir-fry for 1 further minute. Tip the cooked rice into the wok and stir-fry for 1–2 minutes or until the rice is mixed with the meat and prawns, using chopsticks to help separate the grains. Sprinkle over soy sauce to taste.
5 Transfer the nasi goreng to a serving platter. Quickly cut the rolled omelette into thin rings and arrange on the top. Garnish with onion and chilli rings and coriander leaves. Serve immediately.

Serves 3–4
Preparation time: about 20 minutes
Cooking time: about 25 minutes

PINEAPPLE FRIED RICE

250 g (8 oz) long-grain rice
750 ml (1¼ pints) water
4 tablespoons vegetable oil
I garlic clove, crushed
125 g (4 oz) ham, cubed
I carrot, diced
4 tablespoons raisins
¼ green pepper, cored, deseeded and diced
¼ red pepper, cored, deseeded and diced
4 tablespoons Thai fish sauce
I tablespoon sugar
4 pineapple rings, diced
salt and pepper
2 tablespoons chopped coriander, to garnish

1 Put the rice into a sieve and rinse under cold running water, then drain well. Transfer the rice to a saucepan, add the measured water and season with salt to taste. Bring to the boil, stir once then cover the pan and simmer for 12–15 minutes or according to packet instructions until the rice is tender. Turn the rice into a sieve and rinse under cold running water. Set aside to drain.
2 Heat the oil in a wok. Add the garlic and stir-fry until just golden. Add the ham, carrot, raisins, green and red peppers, fish sauce and sugar and stir-fry for 5 minutes. Add the rice and pineapple, season with pepper and stir-fry for a further 5 minutes.
3 Turn into a serving dish, garnish with chopped coriander and serve immediately.

Serves 4
Preparation time: 10 minutes
Cooking time: 15–20 minutes

TEN-VARIETY FRIED RICE

175 g (6 oz) long-grain rice
600 ml (1 pint) water
3½ tablespoons vegetable oil
1 egg, beaten
175 g (6 oz) skinless, boneless chicken breast, finely sliced
125–175 g (4–6 oz) pork fillet, finely sliced
1 red pepper, cored, deseeded and finely chopped
4 spring onions, finely sliced
2 garlic cloves, crushed
3 green chillies, deseeded and finely chopped
3 tomatoes, chopped
125 g (4 oz) cooked peeled prawns
125 g (4 oz) white crab meat, flaked
salt
cucumber strips, to garnish

SAUCE:
150 ml (¼ pint) Fish Stock (see page 10)
2 tablespoons soy sauce
1 tablespoon caster sugar
2 teaspoons lemon juice
2 teaspoons Thai fish sauce

1 Put the rice into a sieve and rinse under cold running water, then drain well. Transfer the rice to a saucepan, add the measured water and season with salt. Bring to the boil, stir once then cover the pan and simmer for 12–15 minutes or according to packet instructions until the rice is tender. Turn the rice into a sieve and rinse under cold running water. Set aside to drain.

2 Meanwhile, make an omelette. Heat 1 tablespoon of the oil in a wok and, when it is hot, add the beaten egg. Swirl the egg around the wok to form a thick skin. When it is cooked through, remove the omelette from the wok, allow it to cool, then roll it up tightly and slice it finely. Set the sliced omelette aside.

3 Mix all the sauce ingredients in a bowl and set aside.

4 Heat a wok, add another tablespoon of oil and heat until hot. Add the chicken and pork, increase the heat to high and stir-fry for 3–4 minutes or until lightly browned. Remove the wok from the heat, tip the contents into a bowl and set aside.

5 Add the remaining oil to the wok and heat until hot. Add the red pepper, spring onions, garlic and chillies and stir-fry for 2–3 minutes until softened. Add the tomatoes and cooked rice to the wok and stir well to mix. Return the chicken, pork and their juices to the wok and increase the heat to high. Pour in the sauce and toss the ingredients until they are combined, piping hot and the grains of rice have separated.

6 Gently fold in the prawns and crab meat, taking care not to break up the crab too much. Heat through, shaking the wok occasionally, and season to taste with salt and pepper. Transfer the rice to a warmed serving dish, top with thin slices of omelette and garnish with cucumber strips.

Serves 3–4
Preparation time: 25 minutes
Cooking time: 35 minutes

INDEX